SOMEONE ELSE'S STREET

Robbie Burton

HAPPENSTANCE

ACKNOWLEDGMENTS:

Versions of some of these poems first appeared in the following magazines and anthologies: Book of Love & Loss, Magma, Poetry News, Poetry Wales, Smiths Knoll, The Interpreter's House, The North.

Printed by The Dolphin Press
www.dolphinpress.co.uk

First published in 2017 by HappenStance Press,
21 Hatton Green, Glenrothes, Fife KY7 4SD
nell@happenstancepress.com
www.happenstancepress.com

CONTENTS

FORD

The donkey followed me to the ford.
I pointed at the river's grey colour and told him
how it ran orange back in the steelworks days
and trout and limestone turned rusty.

I showed him how, even now, you could scrape a stone
and still disturb red oxide.

The donkey remained silent, eyeing the depth of water.
I told him about the spring that used to bubble
in the lane, clear and cool.

Still he stood. I couldn't fathom his thoughts so,
hitching up my skirt, I crossed the ford.

Behind me a clatter, then a splashing. I called out
The river is mostly recycled rain but he continued
upstream. And though he'd told me nothing, his absence
was a cold draught, cold as the incessant water.

WIRE, THE IMPORTANCE OF

As well as rugby league
the town thought
wire was important.
It stretched and twisted
through four factories
and, in our kitchen, grew hot
inside a sixty-watt bulb.

Nothing was seen of
glass chimneyed oil-lamps.
No methylated spirits spiked
the air.

No-one peeled an apple
with a small penknife
and let its skin drop
onto a pine table top
in a dim circle of light.

FROM

It's a cool day in June.
A magpie in the hawthorn
is collecting blackbird eggs.
Thug. Mum collected
people, me, and her other
adoptee, the man from
Hebden Bridge who lodged
in her front room for over
forty years. He collected
stamps and one day
bequeathed them to me
along with a yellow Fiat 126
and a strong dislike of wrong
prepositions. Especially
the one after different.

MAKING SMOKE

The sand had to be damp
and the tunnel small
as if for a doll's grave.

Best, he said, *to use old newspaper*
showing me how to crumple
and pack it loosely in.

A sharp stick made the chimney hole.
Next came his grin, a struck match
and *whooomph!*

Other skills he kept to himself:
training a searchlight,
scavenging chickens

and how to move through Belgium
clearing up after the troops.

PRAYER

Let *fish* not be my name.
Let the classroom not be
full of well articulated
consonants.

Haddock, Roberta?
              Present, miss.

Twenty years on let me
not meet coiffured women
who say Hello, erm—
and stop.

Let me be Bert
with broken fingernails
and fish-tainted
think-bubbles to pop.

TEMPERING

i

Girl sitting still on a hay bale
forget the pursed lips
and sucked-in breaths
of the town, the *tut-tut*
teaching you silence.

Look at the sky
above the shippon.
That's what your uncle's nod
is saying, his own silence born of
content-with-his-lot.

How green his fields.
How white his geese.
How slow his *pah-pahs*
of pipe smoke.

Girl sitting still on a hay bale,
look at the backdrop
of livid clouds.
Watch for *howzats*
of lightning.
Shriek if you like.
Or sing.

ii
Someone must have said *storm*.
Why else is it just uncle and me
side by side at the top of the field,
him puffing clouds from his pipe
and nodding his head now and then
at a lightning-fork sizzling over the shippon
until there's hardly a gap
between strike and thunderclap.

When fat rain pockles the pond
we stroll to the house where
everyone's hunkering under the stairs,
and I am taller, filled
with lightning and thunder and silence
resistant to any *You should*.

CELLAR

                                    Down here
                          the house's art
                    eries are lagged
                in dust and flaked
            with white dis
        temper. Two
sixty-watt bulbs throw shadows across
tea-chests frivolous with Ralph Reader
and Lloyd Webber. Odd knitting
needles and other promises puncture
a brittle *Guardian*. Perhaps later
'Love's Old Sweet Song' will unroll
itself from the gutted pianola. Think of
its notes streaming through an air-brick,
exchanging dark for twilight,
semiquaver pipistrelles echolocating
snowdrops, primroses, bluebells.
Sated, they'll return to their roost
and settle into 'I Know a Lovely Garden'.
But the matchbox collection
and carved-rose soap prompt no flights
of fancy. They sit in their boxes
motionless and mute, like children
for adoption waiting to be picked.

LISZT'S MEPHISTO WALTZ

bubbled through Welsh washdays like
hot tarmac in Bad Piano Street.

No, that's not right. Steam
and the quarry-tiled kitchen are true
but any jangly discords or whiffs of envy
were mine.

Damn, but my cousin could play.
Passion flew out of the iron-framed piano,
shot through two doorways and found
a route in.

For years I felt it
softening me up for love.
I didn't know iron had flowed in too,
waiting for the day.

FIRST DATE, IMPERFECTLY RECALLED

Your best friend was there.
Your last girlfriend was there.
I think the minister was there too.
Charlie Chaplin was there—
or was it Buster Keaton? Laughter
certainly shifted cigarette smoke
in that all-important shaft of light.
Libido was there. I felt it
somersault when you pressed
your palm against mine.
A cockerel was there and I remember
a brass gong and a half-naked
muscled man. No
maybe that was later on.

A CAVEAT TO GOOD NEWS

is in a caller's pause
before
one more thing

in bands of rain
following a builder's
all being well

in silence
after he says
marry me?
and she says
sorry?

and he hears
yes

LOVE POEM

They asked me to write you into a love poem.
I said I couldn't do it, not knowing enough
about the bend and stretch of your sinews
and why a single hair grew in the middle
of your chest. I wasn't prepared to tell them
about your irises going fuzzy
or the way your face changed shape that time
you were trapped inside a room with strangers
turning you into someone I'd never met.

With you inside a love poem, I said,
music would blast through the words, letting out
bus engine rumble and the *thud-thud-thud* of boats.
Surely they could see that a love poem with you in it
would really be about me.

SOME THINGS WON'T BE
SAID GOODBYE TO

For instance, boats.
I tried saying goodbye to one of those.
To its burbling propeller and ticking kettle.
To the doily of sunlight patched above our bed.

Goodbye I said, marking danger points
on my mind's eye map. Trunk roads crossing
hump-backed bridges. Marinas squaring up
to the west coast mainline.

But people giving me lifts don't follow my rules.
They take roads past sudden canals where
lovers still chat on narrow boat roofs
and fall asleep later in firelight.

WHEN THE PLUMBER DIDN'T CALL,

I worked a damp flannel
over those parts of my skin
a good hot bath
should have taken care of
   bastard!
and I couldn't help thinking
of your plumbing bag
and the way you left
   bastard!
our floorboards uprooted for days.

On the fourth day
I crouched beside the bath
and detached the loose U-bend
from its threads. I emptied it
of slimy hair and foul
   bastard!
   bastard!
water before screwing it back again.

There are things that don't change.
Electricity. Reading in bed.

THE TROUBLE WITH SPACE

It looks so spattered from down here,
in need of a Parks Department gardener
to plant stars and planets in neat rows,
the moon centred like a floral clock.

Meanwhile, in somebody's wardrobe,
tops, jeans and skirts hang in one half
and dust floats free in the other.

That's the trouble with space. Somebody
somewhere will stare at a night sky
and think about chaos and wardrobes.
They'll wonder if the time is right.

BWLCHGWYN

The village
calling itself
Highest In Wales
is nothing
but bumps
on the skyline
except for one
starburst of light
that seems
to be bigger
than roofs.
I don't suspect
wreckers this far
from the coast.
Or a spaceship
so late
in the morning
but it could
be a window
throwing the sun
back in its face—
a quick *ting!*
in the village's grin
before being
cut off by cloud,
or earth spin.

DAWN, LIZARD POINT

They call it a 'picture window' and right on cue
a lighthouse beam enters stage left.
It travels the unbroken sea as a patch
of pale grey and collides with a small blip
at the edge of the pane, a meeting
that briefly sharpens man, paddle, canoe.

I can sense the man's sweat from here, digging
his way through waves in his fight with the tide.
Now he, too, exits. Mist blots out his wake
and all that's left in focus is the frame.

SOLO DECISION NO. 203

Sap. A word often used
by a poet I know.
Kiss. She likes that one, too.
Sap kissed by moonlight.
She's very poetic.

Sap can't be kissed by moonlight,
I say. Her mouth opens
as soon as mine shuts
and her fingers tap-tap
on the table. It *can for me,*
she says.

I pick up a pen
and stare at my notepad.
If a few squiggles of ink
is all it would take

THE KNITTED CAT

Auntie Lou said she'd knit her girls a cat,
a hard task for a woman without skill.
Or girls.

Imagine being her
crying on the floor beside
her mother-in-law's dresser.
No spilt polish.
No broken heirloom.
Nothing bloodied
that her niece could see.

And imagine being the knitted cat,
belly slack with dropped stitches,
head prone to unravelling.

UNCOUPLED

On the day she heard how time had drilled
holes in her husband's mind, splitting

> man-that-was
> from
> wife-that-is

she thought of the boy
who boards the wrong bus
and after three stops
leaps from his seat

> thumpings in his chest
> and ticket in his fist

nothing to do
but rapid eye blinks
as he walks past closed doors
in someone else's street.

BORDER

From the other side of the hedge
a *sh-shh* rustling. It stops
when we stop. Starts
when we start. Hawthorns
grow darker and taller.
Soon there's nothing
but our urgent feet
and that soft insistent rustling.

On her side of the hedge
the cow tugs at long grasses.
She hears nothing
but the *sh-shh* rustle of supper.
She doesn't see fear
place stones in our hands.

MAN OPPOSITE, LONDON EUSTON TO CHESTER

On another day
your personalised Jaguar
might have thinned my lips,
      as would all the Jaguars
        of your brother, wife and sons.

Your frequent air trips to the Caribbean
might have chewed off my thumbnail.
Your fuel-guzzling yacht and three glasses of red
        despite diabetes
certainly would have snapped
my Papermate pencil.

Your views on immigration
        which I must admit
        surprised me, being tough
        on government and kind
        to trapped migrants
bit the inside of my cheek
until I'd digested your words.

On another day
we might not have swapped
        sea and canal boat,
        Harrow and Warrington,
        family-get-together
stories. As it was, we got on rather well
in our Virgin first-class seats
yours last minute,
mine a bargain Advance Single

because we knew, didn't we,
that you, the captain of industry,
and me, the bus driver's daughter,
were our kind of people.

MOLE CATCHER

Me and the dog can sense
the buggers coming.

Four o'clock in the afternoon
and the first tremble of earth.

Five past four I swing the mattock
and up in the air goes the mole.

As soon as he starts to drop
the dog opens his jaw.

Yesterday the minister called.
Tomorrow we're off to the graveyard,

the dog, the mattock and me.
We'll wait till dusk to see

what rises and falls.

Sunday Morning Spiders

by
Victoria Fotios

NeoPoiesis Press, LLC

NeoPoiesis Press
P.O. Box 38037
Houston, Texas 77238-8037

www.neopoiesispress.com

Sunday Morning Spiders
Copyright © 2010

Sunday Morning Spiders by Victoria Fotios
ISBN 10 0-981-99846-1 (paperback : alk. paper)
  1. Poetry. I. Fotios, Victoria

Printed in the United Kingdom

First Edition

For Tom, Joseph, Olivia and Melody

with love

Contents

Introduction

"Language is not the dress but the incarnation of thought"
~Wordsworth

"Without Attention_ to the world outside us, to the voices within us- what poems could possibly come into existence? Attention is the exercise of Reverence for the "other forms of life that want to live"
~Denise Levertov

"Soul clap its hands and sing and louder sing"
~W.B. Yeats

One of the first poems I read by Victoria is included in this collection, titled "Strawberries and Spaceships", it opens;

Sing with me a happy tune
the air is fresh from the night,
our blood is pumped clean
through our pure, red hearts
and our children are safe;
look how lovely are our Joyful diversions

I have read her writing voraciously ever since and had the immense pleasure of coming to know the person this inner song belongs to.

This collection has held me through many readings. Every poem contains an intelligent weighing of word to emotion, an encapsulating of experience in language with a strangeness that I have come to know as the poet's signature. There is a gentle revelation that comes with the gift of another's carefully crafted vision; with these poems, there is not a sense of the hypocrisy of a vicarious experience, there is a sense of shared consequence. Her words draw us into a world where a certain shaping of the imagination is required to enter the portal.

Her poems are confessional, yet they contain enough ambiguity and allusion to engage the intuitive and unconscious, enough gesture and sensation to draw the reader fully into the poem with flared nostrils and salivating mouth open to the full resources of language. Once there we are met toe-to-toe, nose-to-nose with a controlled anger, sharp wit, a subtlety and a spatiality which truly sings through the words, through the spaces between the words. Polarities are shuffled closer together with subtly evocative qualifiers, such as in "Corner Café," one of my favourite pieces; linguistically spare, the tension lies in lines such as "Our eyes met/ and I acknowledged the dimness/ of her gaze" and "She saw it/ and her mouth/ widened" It is this macro focus, this shift of scale to the most minute detail, with the utmost polite restraint, that creates the tension in these poems.

Her poetry is suffused with a gentle reverence for people, for beauty of place and circumstance; even if filtered through the simulacrum of the cultural representation constructed around her, the undercurrents of sensuality, of slippage, of the strata below the surface, barely perceptible and absolutely flawed.

This is a generous collection, it grows within, expanding outward, in tones of light and dark; one voice sings and louder sings and others will dance in response.

I finish with the words of the poet herself from "The Parcel":

I did not keep one for myself
I have my own Words,
my own Truth
my own Darkness

Amanda Joy

Pegs

I have no right to be amused.
I am the one standing naked
with a tea pot in my hand;

but I cannot chase the twist from my mouth
as I watch my neighbour
co-ordinate her clothes pegs
to her washing.

So careful is she
that I think she cannot be happy
but, this soothes her
and who the hell am I to wonder
if it reveals a mind and heart
unfulfilled?

It's half past 11 in the morning.
I have been awake since the fox nudged my door.
I have not washed the night from me,
have not evacuated the bed of me,
not so much as opened the French doors
for fresh air.

She is happy with her rainbow of laundry.
I make my tea,
walk past my wash hamper;

I don't need clothes today
anyway.

A Fox in My Curtains

The air was
so densely polluted.
Rest demanded ventilation, so
I dared to risk the creeping urban dangers
and opened ajar my city doors.
Restlessly, I continued tilted
on slumber through the next
two grey hours.

At six,
disturbed by an insistence,
a snuffling knock and pull on the curtain trails,
I saw the Fox, newly curious.
He had found an opening
that had not been before
for him to explore and
nosed his way in,
"Hey, hey! Out you go Foxy!",
and reversed
only briefly and benignly snared.

He left me strangely delighted
at the attempted intrusion.

But no, he'd not gone yet;
his determined brick snout
poked in again, just to be sure.

I had to demur,
a fox in the bedroom made no sense for either of us.
"No, no, no!"

Convinced,
he continued his rounds,
a plaintive air I fancied on him now.

If he was truly injured
I couldn't say.
He has not returned.

While the Washing Blows (Pegs II)

I note they clipped the river bank;
cut open and exposed,
detritus from both road and river
in the stubby shave of the nettle beds.

It's a lovely day
and humanity crowds on the pub benches,
feet buried in tidal mud,
mouths sunk in London Pride;
the odd ice bucket waves a smoky bottle,
Pimms jugs blush with embarrassment
at their unfashionably late arrival.

I push the pram on.
She's asleep,
my Lily love.
A good baby.

Towards the bridge,
a man is suspended on the stubble,
his demure plaid shirt
belies vagrancy;
the broadsheet napkin
rises on his belly,
and he hugs the empty bottle,
a Sancerre.

I roll the pram over him.
Sleeping Lily's eyes flutter
but she is a good baby.

My stomach speeds as I spy,
a rat and a pigeon
in the final scuttle
of a to-the-death struggle:
the mythological beast is prone winged
and worm tailed,

my throat turns over as the sunlight gleams
on the oily fur of the victor.

Lily cuddles her bunny,
she loves to chew his ears.

Lovers straddle the jetty wall,
legs swing-a-swing-a-swing.
Beer bottle erect,
I recognise her unclothed shoulder
from this morning's periphery,
as I sailed Lily's bedclothes
from a harmony of pegs.

The sheets swung as my hair once did,
before I hacked out the choking hazard,
my brush still misses it.

I see her laugh under her hat
and she cups the face of the boy
who was not there
when I heard her screaming:
the walls shook as
her door thundered in its frame;

but things move on,
and so do I.

La-la Lily wakes,
such a good baby,
her nap is done,
and it looks like rain.

Lying in Bed

Laying in bed
can't you hear the bum note
in my "Oh, Oh, Oh!"?

Pre-programmed incorrectly to smooth your ego.

Simple physics tells me
if you feel good
you will love me.

Simple paranoia informs me
I must not let go.

My female deception
avoids me loving me.

You, so selfishly generous,
tell me you can take on the world

but I am here
right now
lying in bed
so that you will love me again.

Shared Garden to Rear

I hate my neighbours garden.
Its vomit of reds, shrieks of cerise and
regimental geraniums.

Good God!
Chrysanthemums!

I know that he too is perturbed by my half of the plot,
divided by the land registry jot.
He must wring his hands over the dappled shade,
the scruffy deck,
a place for dining,
un-specifying,
wining and whining,
not admiring.
His half is the age that I wish to avoid,
our borders are generational.

Geraniums!

Roast Chicken

The bone cracked gravy
is spiked with lemon thyme
and the dregs of a slightly
uninteresting Chablis.

The salad bowl is smeared
with the cut side of smoked
garlic.
Now, oil, vinegar and
Dijon mustard
amalgamate on the tip
of an enthusiastic fork to
coat the gathered herbs
and nasturtium.

Catch the buttery sizzle of
tiny, fresh dug potatoes;
oh staple sustenance!
It could be dauphinoise
or sauté or, oh please!,
sticky, Sunday roasted;
so long as it nurtures
and comforts
it will often be
the best bit.

The much loved bird
steams in it's crispness,
silently seething with the
promise of deliciousness,
pricking the nostrils of the
neighbours, teasing them
to be invited friends.

This is my tavola,
I would share it
and the wine.

Gentle tendrils of honeysuckle
will wind around us,
the candles will flicker
as we tell the stories that
we are deep into the
warm hush of the night.

The Library

Two weeks after he left.....

Eight coats of overpriced
eggshell finally imparted
the dusty permanence
I sought from my alcoves.

Satisfied, I brought my tomes
forth and spent a happy afternoon
sorting and stacking the books that
fed my soul, heart and belly.

My American poets rubbed
each other up the wrong way, while
Oscar and Spike took up
far too much room.
The Russians approved of their
proximity to the hearth
and uninterrupted view of the street.
Meanwhile, the Brits said little
but looked pained.

The cooking and travel
sections beamed with nurture.
The quiet evocation of
shortbread winters
and caramel summers
so excited me
that I whisked two volumes
directly to the kitchen,
intent on laying a table
for long tentative friends
that I may soothe our
reintroduction with
unctuous preparations.

A friend called and assured me
that to have sections
demonstrated a calm mind.
Others worried and those
that loved me
teased.

I smiled.
The shelves were voracious
enough to leave room
for more
words, words, words.

……. My home, finally,
became my own.

Terence

Crumpled lines of sparse corduroy
bag silently at the hip,
a gentle echo of the flesh beneath.
No keys or coins jangle in the pocket rims
just some bird seed
is all.

He carries a scent of must
with scruffed aplomb.
There is a dingy dignity
in his acridity.
Elegant fingernails stubs are
tallow yellow, defined with lines of grime
earned from the caress
of the vegetable beds.

They all know
he sleeps here
in among the muddy plenty
of the Tot Hill allotments,
he tends the espalier pears and the dahlias
as his own.

Only one objection
was ever lodged
against his lodging,
but the quiet, kindly weight of
"Let him be",
crushed the loss of a few potatoes
from a plot owners wife
who preferred
her Jersey Royals flown in,
if she was honest.

That he feeds the birds
keeps them from the raspberry canes,

what matter if his fingers are stained
from his picking his pudding?
That he warms himself
by the burner smoking with
bay hedge clippings,
disperses a pastoral mystery
in this too urbanscape.

He does not speak
but reveres the onion boxes,
allium altar with promises
of soup.

The robins
the starlings
the foxes
the council, for now,

let him be.

Honesty of Alcohol

It was not the tears that hurt me
but the silence,

Blind fear choked me as I lost sight of him,
of myself.
Quiet anger silenced me and
suspended me above the final precipice.

interrupted, only briefly,
by the honesty of alcohol
and the rain.

The wine told him I hated him,
that my flesh was no longer his
and crawled away under his touch.
I poured another glass,
the honesty of alcohol
freed me.

The rain,
still warm with Summer's dying.

And the rain,
still warm, washed our faces,
providing sincerity to my dry cheeks.
Autumn bore the expectancy of death.

We'd never expected "forever"
or even to carry on past the excitement,
fights were fun and tumbled us into bed.

Another hope dashed,
my stomach clenched
as I saw in the broken mirror
he was not for me,
nor I for him.

Now that we had drawn blood out of passion,
our end was near.

Now a death hung in the air.
Now a death hung in the air.

I had to stop myself from hitting her
so I used words,
cruel,
hate filled
words,

If he had just spat upon me
at least I could wipe my cheek,
physical bruising would heal.

she heard the venom,
she tasted it,

His words, words, words
drained down the back of my throat.
The vomit mechanism suspended,
I savoured his defense of hate
and the poison welled over.

And then the tears came,
And then the tears came,

And then the silence,
And then the silence,

And the rain.
And the rain.

Lila

Unbridled joy and sustenance
caught mid-flight, you are
our bursted, apple blossom.

The world attempts to reign
you in with complexity
but your gossipy response
marks you out,
a survivor.

From the moment we met,
we have been in love.

You liked our conversations,
revelled in the babbling
conundrums we constructed
together, in an attempt to
un-sense certain sensibilities,
and
put to one side,
any generational divide.

Your jaggedy, fresh soul
bristles with facets.
Mine is muffled by nurture
but we meet
in the middle,
my marvellous muddle.

Just watching you eat,
"I love my food!",
gorging and wasting not a
hairs breath of kinesis,
tumbling, firebird girl.

Railton Road on a Sunday Morning

A few moments of quiet before we recollect
the battle.
The gentle hip shake of reggae echoes
as we roll together
across the floor
and our eyeballs
jolt at the memory.

Tentative elation flips and warms our
stomachs.
A fag packet drops from the air
so we light up to exchange the smoke
from the George
with a more welcome acridity.

In the far corner of the room,
the fag fairy farts and mumbles that his arm hurts.

The rumble of voices in the street below
is different and muted,
you can hear it over the surge of the firehoses
but
no call to arms today my comrades,
today is for reflection.
We tumbled the State
by pissing on our own doorstep.

Sunday Morning Spiders

Exiled from the bed folds,
there must be time to soak the sheets.
Air dry and remake,
crisp edges and tidy corners.

Friday night debris
spread into Saturday afternoon.
A flotsam of joy,
she preserved the mementos for as long
as she could;
but tripped over the forks and magazines
three times too often.

The orchid, selected for its longevity
and harmony,
is the wrong blush of pink;
it clashes
the fascist upholstery,
but hides the tea stains of an earlier occupation.

Spiders come in from the early cool,
as the sharp shouldered girl
scribbles with her forehead,
seeking to transfer deathless prose
to a page with recipes for duck in the margins.

For the third day in a row,
she will waste her make-up,
only attracting
unwanted attention.

Fancied vanity is removed and
channeled through her pen now.
It will endure much longer
than her smile.

Her mother chided
as she lifted the children,
*You will break your back
with that burden of love.*

Her mouth twists as she adds
early figs to the mallard.

Intact Lane

I have walked this lane
all my life.
It is nothing more
than an ancient cut through,
from home to friendly places,
more convenient and friendly
to those it knows.
A daylight rat run with
ivy tumbled walls and leaf dusted gutters.
My lane.

Familial bonds have returned me
and the night finds me here again,
emphatically stamping out
arguments outside my grasp
as I did in my only-just-woman form.
Why it is here still,
this twenty five year old echo of
the anxious to please child?

My head feels the same,
nothing has changed.
I am repelled and propelled here
to find that crack in time to crawl into
and wait.

It is dark
but there is not a shadow that I cannot recognise
with a hello nod.

The tree crouched tunnel leads
to the orchard of my grandma's dear acquaintance.
I amble, damply hushed to my apple tree
and lift my arms for it
to sweep me to its shoulders.

My jacket shines and
I am strange fruit;
a displaced urbanite,
home for a moment.

The cradled firmament
inspires my veins to rush and pump.
Sinister breezes curiously finger
my clothes and hair.
I am calm,
I know their grip is that of butter
hitting the bars of my skin.

We are content,
Tree, sky and I.
We swing together again, to
postpone the moment I must leave.

Bathroom

Though you
absorb my every thought,
I quite like the cup of tea
you leave me
on the nightstand.

I mull quietly,
over its steam,
the outline
you left in the doorway.

Though I want
to sink my teeth into your shoulder,
assimilate you,
I enjoy hearing your pad
through the rooms I am not in.

I laze, cushion quiet,
head bobbing with thoughts
and my lip sticks
to the teacup.

My eyes tip and drop,
a profound quietness brushes the air,
I smile in anticipation
as I hear the flush.

Sleeping on the Beaches of Donegal

While waiting for life to begin,
I constructed another from spit,
sent the feelers out, some took
and now I cannot un-dig them.

When you left with my friends
to let me holiday with humiliation,
I sacked continents to find a place
I could bury my need to slice.

In the pit, the treasure chest is manacled.
I sketched a map to it in my unconsciousness
even as I brushed the sand from my hands.

As a child,
I am often told,
I sought adoption on beaches and in shopping areas.
Magnetic kindness would clamp me,
I would reach to hold the hands of strangers,
ready to attach my tiny love spring
to a wider smile.

Gypsy daughter!
Where was my loyalty to the labour pains?
But I fell to this earth
and could transmute as I chose.

How hard, hard for my parents,
hand feeding such ingratitude.

Little has changed;
you hold the mirror,
I rub honey into it.

Ham and Eggs

Deep in my womb
gestates the question;

Yes/No/Yes/No/Yes/No.

No.

I consider roping off my areas for tourists,
provide hard hats and hand rails;
Come, come!
admire my stalactites.

The stagnant pool of my sex
glows green.
I screw up my face to see future reflection,
don't dare question it
nor comment upon the murk.

Yes.

Let's talk about the maybe baby.
Please,
bear in mind the time.
Shrink wrapping is for hams,
not families.

Open up this one with me to
see our future swaddled,
cooing,
now cooling.

Buckets

The land is dry-sunken and falls away seeking a frame.
The practiced prettiness of the estuary
is destroyed by the organ pipes of industry.
Once misted shores are now slugged with effluent
and the sigh of the chimneys is a testament,
grieving for beauty lost.

Washed further up is the vandal tattooed mansion.
It wears its history as a moth-chewed Duchess,
eyes a smudge of kohl and lips a bloodless slash,
she fondles her rags of pearls.

On the rolled tongues of her lawns
play your children and you.

I sit, with her at my back, on a burning bench.
My worry bead book makes me furtive
but I feel the glare and penetration of neon.
You play on, unknowing, yet are all drawn to me,
as I to you.

Now, here you all are, buckets of bugs swung and thrust
towards me;
pride in the bead spattered, hawthorn bouquets.
An enormous spike bursted chestnut is millipede scarved,
we chuckle at his affronted, tumbling crawl.

The babies bubble with joy
and it drags across my sternum.

The tiniest of robins ticks the hour,
I may stalk you to the park
but no further.

The Parcel

Uniformly packed,
it contained five brown skinned parcels.
My hands floated and would not connect
as I tore and unpeeled
to expose the black jacketed Bibles,
each fragrant with newness.

Hotly branded gold,
labeled to inform me that they were Holy,
demanding worship.
Here, they told me,
is the Word,
the Truth
and the Light.

I divided up the bounty,
each tome reserved for a friend.
My offerings would be received with relief,
the hierarchy of my regard affirmed.

I did not keep one for myself.
I have my own Words,
my own Truth
and my own Darkness.

Chip Wrapping Disclosure

Nothing for me,
thank you.
They put vitamins in my body cream
so I no longer have to eat.
Pull up a seat and order what you like,
the bar will be with us presently.

In the offices of television centre,
Smoker's corner seems chic
but I coughed too loudly
and was exposed as a geek
when I couldn't drag humour
from caged hamsters.

No please, please
have something
that I may have second hand digestion of,
you don't mind if I smoke,
was not a question.

Hold out your hands
as I drop snippets from up high,
watch you juggle with a subtext
that I have carefully erased
after too many altercations
with my own words on your page.

I know the drill,
you will compliment my still
girlish presentation and elegant attire,
then subvert it with the punctuation of my age;
harsh context to any admiration.

Looking good is so common these days,
but you will only see my lipstick,
not my message.

11:45 PM

The garden is dark.

It sinks with
it's own weight
and the cloak of night drags
the trees
deep towards the core,
sucking down, down, down.

He floats.

He is suspended.

He tells me via satellites
that his skin is ablaze,
burning with firestorms
that rage across the Sun.

He itches
with the prickle of electricity
drawn and conducted
from the Universe.

He is frightened,
but this could be Happiness.

He says that it thrashes
and snakes.
The cable is live, sparks illuminating
the sky for one thousand kilometers;
how is he then to earth it
without it juddering his heart
to a standstill?

His fear shocks him,
but this could be Happiness.

Strawberries and Spaceships

Sing with me a happy tune,
the air is fresh from the night,
our pumped blood is clean
through our pure, red hearts,
and the Children are safe;
look how lovely are Our joyful diversions.

On the mountains of Africa, the snowfields endure.
Perhaps the poisonous grasp of human sewage
is not so bad after all.
Maybe there is more jungle than we could ever need,
the Amazonian dumps are benign,
and the Children will be safe.

You tell me that we will live in peace for one hundred years,
pick strawberries and fly in spaceships.
We will take the Children and we will keep them safe.
I pull down a peach from Our tree,
dismiss, for now, the oily shadow in the lens
and welcome the blessed complacency.

Sunday

My garden is planted with seeds.
I dibble and furrow,
so sure of germination,
crouching and cramping over my babies.

Fight!
Fight, through the dark crumble of the Earth
plucky little sprouts.
You will be beautiful,
and so loved.

He swings a hello
on the gate of my madness,
secured just with a daisy chain.
It seems right that he is here
in this evening.
The sleepy sun paints us pink
as we survey the beds.

Later,
when I told him the truth,
his scream clashed and thumped.
I couldn't find the trapdoor in the couch
to get out.

Children

We are still angry.
See,
see it hacked and scribed deep in our soul bones,
all three submissive to your subversion
and cleverly
molded to accept full blame.

We grew into our taught faults
and found others who echoed
your life-long assertions
and affirmed our total pointlessness
in order to elevate themselves.

My Sister and my Brother,
like me,
are still identified by our faded tattoos,
brands issued by the regime
under which we all suffered.

Now,
years later,
we require a thousand other voices
for us to hear
we are worth loving.

But we only wanted it from you.

We are lucky.
Real love came,
removed the off switch from our grasp.
Our whealed backs will heal.
No one ever can
remove the scars from yours.

Dust

The tentative hollow
in the landscape
indicates the
position of the deletion.

A spiral of vultures
leads the crowd
to the spectacle
of the widows,
out crying each other,
scrambling over the
dead bones.

Here,
somewhere
is the affirmation of the
importance
of each
to him.

One is suttee
the other will live on,
alone.

They demand
proof that one's grief
is real grief;
big,
epic,
hounding,
bleeding grief;

where the other is merely
slicing onions
in the rain.

Kizzy

Beyond verbal,
though we talked this up.

Let's get close
and exchange,
so we feel good and connected.

If it is right,
our stomachs will curdle,

if not, then hell,
it was worth a try
to locate the fabled drop,

that thing that makes the Universe stop,

and feel.

So sorry,
it just didn't mean anything to me.

You had a mountain to climb
but I smiled at you as I issued the warning.

Trainers Not Wings

The path is compacted by sub-urban footfalls
that thunder along it all times of the day.
Each of us has a time,
but mainly, like a harras of horses,
Saturday mornings.

My legs strapped on,
I launch myself.
To walk is to crawl in a shell
and I must catch up with my hare brain.

Winning is not important,
but I race nonetheless.

My Sister's legs twitch under the table,
they are as dogs at the door, leads smiling.
Claws rattle and bodies boom along the hall.
Let's go!
There are hills and fields and rivers full of fish.
Dinner is over.

I run by the river,
lung burst crimson.
With democracy, I hope, I nod and gasp
to those I flash by.
Some meet me halfway,
most clamp eyes downward.
Ignore the running woman, and the sleeping man in
his bundle of clothes and newspaper.

The dogs juggle along,
the herons pose,
the skulls glide above the fish.
I shudder as the river bed seethes with bathing starlings.

I run while I can.

Nearly returned I come upon the ancient lady.
Wheelchair poised, almond eyed, punk-shocked hair.
Lovely, hunched lizard.
We each raise our hands
and I skittle on.

Cohabitation

It was a shock
so long unspoken.
My asking,
your acquiesce.

I nibbled you a key from my fingernails.

You came,
hung your shirts,
your boots
took root.

These items and I now share abandonment.

In my fridge is the promise of intimacy,
but the chops spoilt
so I drank the wine,
picked the wax from the table,
wondered about the weekend.

I throw my head back as I recall
you didn't even leave me a bath-ring,
but your socks hang like tongues in my hamper.

Perhaps when one goes missing,
you will live here.

Cracks

So it is this way.
Eternally so.
Though I have my hands caught behind me,
a spread of innocence,
I did push until it tottered and fell to earth,
smashed and dashed across the wood paneled floor.

I am comfortable with the splinters
as they glitter in my fingers.

Hypnotized by the liquid spread,
I am vaguely aware that it will stain
and welcome the permanence of the scar.

In pieces it is manageable.
The expectation eroded,
I hold it easily and toss the cooling fragments
one palm to another,
allow the snip of the edges bring me peace.

As a perfect whole
it was too easy to lose it all;
damaged goods don't travel so far.

Flying Saucerless

Low tops let me fly over
cracked paving stones.
I miss the elegant tottering
of vertiginous shoes
but today,
I am scooting for coffee and news,
disguised as a twelve year old boy.

I sit at the edge of the pavement
at a table freckled with sugar and half-moon cup rings.
I take my too-milky coffee gargantuan,
wonder yet again what to do with the spoon
added to sweeten the bitter Arabica;

I take it as it is,
stir meditatively anyway.

The café portico is secluded by red taped scaffold
framing it out to the commute laden road.
I sequester the scene and imagine palazzo.
My cloister mates argue in Italian,
earnestly prodding
each others nerves with espresso cups.

I cannot keep them out
of my ears
so sketch them in composition;
my words outline their slip on shoes
and leather jackets.
Their cigarillo fingered gesturing
mesmerises me from under my hat.

My coffee goes cold.

Joe

Today,
I felt the press
of your little head
into my hip
as we casually walked on.

Your sisters scampering
ahead of us,
your Daddy,
connected to all of us
by the constant,
invisible thread,
though I know not
where he
stood
at that, exact moment.

The baby-bear
pressure
made me
gasp, as if
your fresh born
fingers
had just captured
my thumb.

In this first moment,
I held you
and we sewed
the seed of our permanent,
fledgling love.

Tavola

Papa,
I understand
your need to billow
the tablecloth and
delight us with dishes
to crowd and elbow
our way through,
beneath a sun dappled bower.

The dogs and the children
tumble and swing,
you want a rabble of Italians
smiling at you.

Mama,
I understand
you want a Hollywood staircase
with full camera crew,
to record and broadcast
how we all love you.

You want the envious applause
and the photo proofs catching
us all smiling.

Love is pointless in private.

My friend walked backwards
to collect the dust from his boots
while I sang to my scars,
a dedication
to my growing pains.

The table was empty,
the lens was empty…

Mr. Toad

I wanted horsepower,
so sent yesterday's creatures for recycling
and created a stable of technology.

The glossy flanks of my loved apparatus
allow me automotive notoriety.
Ruminative grazing was not for me,
I hate manure, so
kill the roses.

I have my license on a piece of elastic
in the glove box.
I do not
trot,
nor care a jot
for the law.

Oh, let's go for a burn
my pretty friend!
We can spin, destruct and disturb
the peace.

We will fly too fast to catch frowns
from our elitist machine,
and what fun it is to laugh at those
who pitch into the hedgerows.
It's their look out,
so lookout!!!

My dear, you look quite green,
almost as I.

Tone-deaf

I wanted a butch red,
so decanted it into a tumbler.

I recalled how you teased
my Champagne over ice
in those tea glasses
from Essaouria.
Christ!
Couldn't you just enjoy it?

The radio rumbled on
un-listened to, until
it nudged me with a story
of two young violinists,
who,
faced with abatement,
took their lovely strings elsewhere.

Apparently,
the walls of the Mancunian flat
were not as thick as the ears of their neighbours,
nor as dense as the local council abdicators.

I fancied inviting them to live above me,
defrosted the Reblochon;

Manly.

Things I Recalled on Waking

Light sliced in between
the squeezed crush of my eyes.

The dancing bear
of the preceding night,
wore a ruff,
smarting eyes
and a black gouged nose;
I blinked him
and his pain away.

I wondered if that was me on the table,
or was I underneath it,
wondered from the coins on the floor
if I could eat today.

I recalled the tiny child
locked in the parlour,
I wondered if I loved her.

I remembered the moment
of true love,
wondered where it went.

Heaven sent
coffee smells
reminded me,

just before
I wondered where you had gone.

Treading Softly

Whatever I think that I am
is now opposite.

I am changed because of you.
You re-made and
smoothed my rumples,
helped me stack the detritus
into the bowels of my
straining wardrobes.

All will be fine until
we need to find a pair of shoes.

The moment I
bit down on the dark caramel
of your shoulder,
sweetness coated my mouth
with a smile that will
never leave my eyes,
though they sizzle with salt
water at so many lost years.

I dance your wishbone
into my hips,
rejecting any inference that
I was at any point,
A charlatan,
A cheat,
A woman;
A failure of my breeding
and my sex.

The correction of my path
to be played out
in the void between
reality and the ethereal spread
of my peers,

should they welcome
my pampas transmutation
into fingerable edges,
is a question
to be answered
by dead accountants.

I Saw Your Ghost

Big fingered whittling
of Lilliputian gourds,
each one of fingernail proportions,
a tiny ghoulish face
peeping from the empty head.
Is this the size of love?

Pumpkin head
could never be a compliment.

On the edge of my slumber
I rumble along the mattress,
raw from the bite of the sweat soaked
tides of anxiety.

I awake in the middle dream world.
Here in my mezzanine consciousness
sliver of sleep,
I saw your colossus
menace the air above me.

Confusion,
as I feel for the real world
at my elbow,
but the visitation still mushroom clouds above me
and terror writhes and rips through my throat.

Seconds yawn red
as the Ghost vapourises and
you wake in time to collect
my sobbing bones.

You cough a lullaby to my brittle,
snapping teeth,
breathe coolness into my lungs,
soothe me back.

But,
I saw your Ghost

and now watch for its return
with taut, matchstick eyes.

The Afternoon Kitchen

Curiosity and jealousy
is sapping the flow
of creativity.

Idle drifts of phrases
collect in pools around the nostrils,
but cannot sustain art,
however abstract the intent.

The fingers
are content
to prattle and rattle,
capturing and pouring
conscience into dark ink.

Would that the clouds
were not so dark
and the leaves and birds
would not flip black and silver
and silver and black,
indecipherable from one another,
they scatter and disperse constantly.

The stripped bones of the crumbling year
are bleached by early ice.
All sounds are air sharpened
into high relief.

There is no need,
as yet,
to yellowy illuminate
the kitchen table,
scattered with ten things
that have not been done
yet this week.

Catharsis will come
as the bladder empties,
the elemental soup
will whirl away,
nothing more
will be created today.

Dirty Bar Room Brawl

The thrown drink soaked her knickers
right through to the skin.
Her wild punch too unfocussed
to make substantial connection
with the leer of the pony tailed girl,
an empty glass in her hand,
grinning gorgon,
a bitter mouthed,
lip smeared,
tart.

A flung beer the perfect
attack and defense,
insulting and injurious vessel.

Humiliation spat out
venomous phlegm
and the door staff arrived
to drag her out by her
new halter necked top.
She objected, so the
police were called,
much better than beating a woman.

Men watched impotently,
aroused by a cat fight,
amused by the drag of the nails,
the rip of the teetering,
too-made-up,
hell hounds.

The long bath,
rollers and
precision cosmetics,
became a pitiful memory.

Her seduction technique
was saved for a fumble
in the alley, with
no-one she knew.

Steak Sandwich

You blame me for finding you out
and fucking throwing you out,
yet not wanting to.

This was nothing that I wanted,
I reject it with every seething fibre
and yet, what foolishness
would carry on with your
constant threat of violent humiliation?

You have destroyed
the last gasp trust in a truth
that I grabbed as I left the house.

You double crossed and wired lies,
then forgot where you buried them
so, that however lightly I skipped,
they could be tripped
and blow my leg off,
blow my heart out
and my faith away.

I scraped the sandwich from the ceiling
that I began to prepare
in my mind
hours before
you declined to eat it.

Waste of meat,
waste of me,
wasted.

That I writhed
and spat
and cracked the air,
raining my anger in heartbroken
body blows,

you could neither accept
as consequence,
nor fair comment.

My actions
and reactions
shored you up onto higher ground,

you look down,
I look down,
it's over.

Grandfather

You hate.
It was in your generational DNA
to mistrust,
yet you watched the back of others,
as ordered.

The Empire taught you sympathy
for the very views that were to be stamped out.
The selection for a hint of darkness on the lip
to be thereafter identified by the ochre patch.
No! This could not to be tolerated
and yet, those were not the reasons
you went to War;
that absolution was a by product
of the battle for King and for Country.

To be grown tall and blond,
a reflection of God's light,
like yourself,
seemed logical.

To be dark
is to be as the
shadows of the abyss
beneath the Earth.

Bleak pits of pitched bodies were dug and
the cursed generation was stamped out in unison.

You had one hundred names for it,
you would not deny it,
but it was not the main agenda,
nor the reason for your colours.

No, you fought for pomp and for home.
There was no altruism in war back then,

none now,
if we are honest.

When the fighting stopped,
you fought on,

your family
your neighbours,
yourself.

You instilled fear and respect in
your tiny Grandchildren,
who saw the child still in there
and loved him.

Tautened to hear the clock
striking the lost hour,
you dreaded the day
we would not hear
your pied pipes,
and hated us for it.

Hardback

Rigid seating
broke the back of the slumped incumbent.
Soft mechanisms have seized,
leaving nothing but
a high perch for the leg bowed,
slouch hipped,
blister lipped
girl.

Disapproving pupils trace the contour
of her inverted spine,
propped by the numb hinge joint.
Her face drips and pours out through her fingers,
leaving the desk a melted pool of friendly faces
and skeletal planting.

Around her the office moves,
she remains still,
her mentality cocooned within a deep silence.
High force fields of ignorance protect her from
her colleagues discomforted irritation.
They shift as they hump her cadaver,
she herself has already collapsed
under the weight of her own inability
to communicate,

that muscle is cut and withered away.

The torch is set to the pyre,
but the crowd pissed on it
to save her from escape,
leaving only acrid, ammonic smoke
to drift,
now that the spark is gone.

How are you?
How was the weekend/kids/holiday?

Fine.

Dolores Dislikes Buffet Parties

And there it was,
a cacophony of cutlery
deafening the rose petal
Pavlova
and tumbling
an artful display of grapes.

The swoosh of the linen
roared
as she mashed her way through
various potato salads.

Three kinds of bread got beaten
for no reason
anyone watching could muster.

Mustard spat biliously
across the lemon rolls
and pools of sweet cherry chutney.

A crumbed ham
blushed and bled at the bone.
The devilled eggs grew wings
and the room dripped with
the stench of a fine Camembert.

Finally,
as the rooms' stomach rumbled,
the salmon flan
got flattened.

Corner Café

The coffee
pooled coldly upon the
red of the table and
soaked deeply into my shirt sleeve.

The café, sourly grimy,
swirled in a mist of condensation
that offered neither respite nor comfort
from the down pour I had escaped from.

The booth opposite contained
a lady, who gummed the rim
of her over sweetened tea cup
taking turtle-esque sips of the hot
liquid, before retreating back against
the torn leatherette banquette.

Our eyes met
and I acknowledged the dimness
of her gaze.

A sudden horrific recognition
of this as a future reflection
retched me towards the door
into the safe, wet gleam of the
street.

I turned to see that
I had left my umbrella on my seat,
it lay, benevolently offering itself to
all but me.

She saw it
and her mouth
widened.

Journey

Fine fingered hands drip
disconsolate languidity
from the opened train door
window.
Her eyes flicker in time
with the racing horizon.
She sees the light seasoning
of England,
the dots of sheep,
the punctuative bothys and
scratches of agriculture.

She reaches out to pull in a
passing cloud and, returning
to her seat, knits it
softly in to her discontent.

The putter of the carriages
lacks rhythm and
tunnel after tunnel
pop her ears
uncomfortably.

She is half aware of
the pickled scent of open
cans of beer and
crisp smeared businessmen,
on their way to somewhere else
from yesterday

Her knee grazes a mushroom
of chewed gum under the table
and she wonders at the spit
that adhered it.

Her umbrella rattles
at her ankles

and she attempts a discreetly
fumbled rescue.
Her destination comes thirty moments
hence and she is throat clenched
with an anxiety to
exit un-noticed.

Yesterdays Under-where

How is it
you find it so
easy,
easy
to slip on another skin,
pull it in?

Yet I see
you squirm so
as the
shame rain
descends
to cool the hot
headed passion
of the borrowed
bedstead.

Someone else
will fold
your clothes.
Someone else
will dispose
of the evidential
sheets,
but no one else
will take you home
but you.

This sad regret
is pointless,
consent is subjective,
judgement is suspended,
absolution is not needed.

It will all diminish
in a day or so,

leaving you free
to do it
again.

Cold

A pane of glass seemed to be floating upon
the pool surface,
so smooth and ripple-less that
it should have been human forged,
planed by a master,
rather than petrified by the night.

It was perfectly fashioned from
the hush of the air,
cold, quiet and still as granite,
flawless in execution,
a shimmering rink for fairy skates,
or a pane to replace the broken window of a
winter palace.

Here was the coldest of cold candy
to crack chattering teeth.

A satisfactory snap greeted my
curious finger,
Obese air bubbles beneath bumbled
to the surface
and gurgled their escape.

The ice was broken,
I laughed and glided on.

Christy

Passing time with you,
happily prone upon the silty beds of grass,
we watch cloud puppetry play above
in the melted mirror of your eyes.

Your child face radiates heath and innocence,
a revered combination
that quells my anxiety for you
as you go toward the world.

Your good humour acts as
a force field of kindliness,
keeping the love close and the
nonsense where it belongs.

That we breathed the same
frosty oxygen each Christmas morning,
that we saw your first snow
together,
that I carry your golden heart
with me,
these things,
we things,
continue.

Tinnitus

Hollow souled,
she still believes the hole in her own hype;
constantly despairs in her
own lack of substance.

She hurries through everything with
fingers jammed in her ears.
Peace is a fear,
the quiet question
in a quiet room is
the enemy of every deceiver.

When in need of amusement, she twists
the splinters in her fingers as
atonement for her lack of pain.

She is passion, collected in a loving hand,
but cooled.
Every empty platform has an
expectation of nothingness
in the moments after the carriages
pull away and yet,
we still sit and wait.

The human child learns and builds
its world from hearsay,
rather than truths
and this is the playground
for her sound bite dialogue,
so expertly honed and pitched to
disrupt the natural rhythm of things
it creates only exasperated love.

Her host is compressed with
self doubt and considers
eviction the final solution.

Only in silence can she be judged,
so she continues to chatter over thoughts,
hides in the clatter and
listens to none.

She cried when her small charge announced he
relied only on himself in a sea of love.
She would give all of herself to not recreate
the noise in him.

Final Days (Urban Methadone)

All the boxes are on the van.

I have wandered to
my garden deck and am
observing the scruffy scuttle
of roses against
black plastic bags, brimming with bottles,
a pile of magazines props up the lazy broom.

My buried smile is stirred by
the loveliness of this urban ramble,
sticky scented by
an Etoile de Hollande
that I over-planted.

Roses, I believe,
make everything beautiful,
even corpses.

My neighbours door stands sentry,
glowering a neat, new red,
the fresh buds of my creepers
feast vampiricly upon it.

In Manhattan, the blossom is fabulous
crammed into the oversized vases
of every bar.

The gothic spread of the city
cranes to admire the
swathe of Central park;
all who enter are consumed with an
impulse to meander, to cycle, to pretend
they are somewhere else, while wanting
nothing other.

Out in the Bronx the gorillas and the
college offices struggle with the humidity,
all they can do is sleep or eat cool
plates of ravioli with basil.

At lunch for three,
my ignorance bloomed daisies,
red tipped from the wine,
as I mis-pronounced everything
I ever knew and
forgot the things
I had yet to learn.
The company was benignly
free of judgements.
Boosted by the generosity of
a richly presented afternoon,
we continued to drink
into the evening and
took ourselves so late to Tribeca,
that we missed dinner
but not the City.

On returning,
I found my family
had grown yet,
kept the space for me open.

Leaving my City by going to another
was never going to work.

Leaving my City for my family,
well that's different,
we make those judgements every day
and for much less.

I uncurl myself from under the pergola,
shabby from honeysuckle,
and walk through the empty
rooms I already left

for others.
A good bottle of Champagne
and a new life waits for them.

The van waits for me;
I lock the door.

Even His T-Shirt Was Cruel

Red.

It is
softly cotton and,
I fondly imagine,
impregnated with his DNA,
his essence woven in through
one day wears,
not possible that it
would be laundered out.

Looking for a nest,
I burrowed and curled into it,
surrounded my heat stroked flesh within it,
grasping for familial connection,
telepathy in the fibres,
shrugging on a substitute
for the absent body.

A thousand raining nights
I shrouded myself,
let it hold me limply
hoping for a rescue,
some teleported happiness.

I found its label, scorpion tailed,
sliced into me,
a bitter reminder
pricking my bare hip.

October

Roughing up the clouds,
the wind surprised us all
with an angry spray of rain.

"It's honking down",
said the geese,
and it was.

I preferred to keep
the darkness
inside and view
the murky relief
of a moss scented sky,
through the freckled window,
that still needed a clean.

Back home,
my sisters
love of fresh air provoked
a stubbornly ajar door,
even in January.

Little Eve asked that
the windows and doors
be shut,
but in vain,
so she sullenly wore
her bobble hat to dinner,
trailing her scarf
and fingers in the beans.

I glow at the memory
and am warm

as the rain scratches the skin
of those exposed to its elements.

Fingernails

Between the stench of
domestic waste and
suburban lavender beds,
is oxygen and rain.

Continuing to count the
days in fingernails
is a habit of old,
the white bloom beneath
the surface being reliable
as any ticking mechanism.

In the dream, her lovers
eyes were put out so not
to distract him from his usual ardour.

To deny him such perspective
was, she believed,
an act of mercy on her part,
it denied his detection
of passions exit,
at least for the moment.

The Thief

I spread my fingers wide so as to
catch the detritus of your mood.
Such self-importance brings with it
a mighty responsibility,
directly tripped wired to your pain.

I would cry as you cry but
you never let me see it.
I fade away, denied my existence
in the damp sorrow of your cheeks.

In coveting your world,
I picked it to shreds.
Now, I crouch alongside you,
scrabbling in the dirt to collect
fragments of the life
you thought was yours.

Beware my help in your
attempt at reconstruction.
I cover and bury the pieces that
you need for that;
you see, I built my happiness
upon everything
you own.

Nick

The coldness of the visceral kick
leaves us gasping
at the wrong, wrong, wrong.
Railing at the illogical and senseless
leaves little room for reason.

The house of your torn family
is pregnant with abandonment
but you are right here, buried
across the road, permanently.

It will be they who move.

Too many tonnes of earth
couldn't extinguish your life force,
nor tuck you in safe
and, with you hovering above
your plot,
I change my mind on the
subject of burial.

Parentis Mantis

Playing, as you do,
with my children,
I am sure that you
do indeed have some
interests at heart.

I will not allow
you to believe that
you are anything but
a tourist here,
mere, fond interloper.
So while they laugh at the
balloons now,
be sure to know
that they will be deflated later.

In my care, the gates
of this family are closed to
you outside supervised hours.
You cannot be surprised,
your outrage is fooling no-one
but the baby
and she will learn.

Trauma Bonding

Too, too common is the
practice of kissing the hand that beats
in time with the quickening drum
within.

All bonds are tied and sealed with
the detritus of blood blows.
That's how to recognise love,
It comes with hand raised and
It's lips begging for a forgiveness,
so freely provided by the adoring victim.

See the chided child,
alone with its oppressor,
bent with the burden
of loving an open sore.

For love is purple, swollen eyes,
bursted lips,
ravaged hips and
there is no easy cure for
such nurtured masochism.

Here have we found a peaceful
companionship "Dear",
but recall that we began
in a flailing mass of wrongdoing;
are we bonded by anything
more than tired rage
and the weeping of
our little ones' betrayed heart?

We are in no position to part,
it must then be forever
so that we never
discard the meaning
of our pain.

Do we love our life?
We tell all, "Yes!"
How lucky.

We believed even as another's
lips provided truth,
as the City craned incredulous
to the claim,
"but I'm happy, very happy"
somewhere near,
a lonely nightingale jeered.

Little Dot

Little Dot
squeezes and
she is
everything
I wanted to be.

Singing in
the evening
garden,
she is
beating out
a lullaby
of tiny

Dot,
dot,
dot.

When foiled,
her whine
is notable
for it's
utter
absence of
discernable
melody.

Later,

we are
transfixed
by the
vast expanse
of her
sleeping
lids.

So changed
Am I
by the small force
of her,
my world
can no
longer be
completed without
her outline.

Dot,
dot.

Little Dot
is mapping
the universe,
backwards.

Dot .
Dot .
Dot..

.

Rain

This morning

the rain blazed uncontrolled.
I crouched into your elbow and listened to its
boots thump along the gutter,
watched the shadows of its march
as they crossed our upturned faces.

I couldn't bear the thought
of hovering along the spray,
into today.

The walls sucked up the light,
leaving them full of smooth, soft grey.
I pulled the sheet over your shoulders
in order that I may conceal
my schizophrenic layers,
just for today.

So we slept a little more
knowing that there can be no choice but to
prepare the children for
when the black things come.

Let us not rip the bedclothes from them in panic,
we can lift and hold them tenderly to suspend the horrors
that threaten at the precipice of the doorstep.
The albatross is not welcome here.
Not today.

Permissions & Acknowledgements

The original version of *Children* was edited by C. Madoch

Original versions of the following poetry appeared in *Online Poetry, Volume One* featuring Victoria Fotios as Poetry Blog Rankings' *Online Poet of the Year 2008*:

Roast Chicken; The Library; Cold Water; Terence; Rain; Bathroom; While the Washing Blows; Sunday Morning Spiders; Intact Lane; Sleeping on the Beaches of Donegal (Boxes 6 & 7); Ham and Eggs (Box 5); Buckets (Box 4); Chip Wrapping Disclosure; 11.45PM; Strawberries and Spaceships; Sunday; Children; Dust; Shared Garden to Rear; Trainers; Not Wings; Cohabitation; Tone Deaf;, Things I Recalled on Waking; I Saw Your Ghost; Steak Sandwich; Hardbacked; Yesterdays Underwhere; A Fox in My Curtains; Lying in Bed; Pegs.

Original Versions of Pegs, Lying in Bed and *A Fox in My Curtains* were published in the *Alabaster and Mercury Journal, Volume 1.*

The Honesty of Alcohol was co-written with Si Philbrook.

Kind thanks to Si Philbrook for his editing and for his friendship; To Dale Winslow for her wonderful encouragement, sense that there needed to be SOME punctuation and fun; To Amanda Joy for greeting my outstretched hand in the early days and for the beer(s) we shared in Paris.

To my family and friends, my undying love, admiration and respect; Thank you.

NeoPoiesis
a new way of making

in ancient Greece, poiesis referred to the process of making
creation – production – organization – formation – causation
a process that can be physical and spiritual
biological and intellectual
artistic and technological
material and teleological
efficient and formal
a means of modifying the environment
and a method of organizing the self
the making of art and music and poetry
the fashioning of memory and history and philosophy
the construction of perception and expression and reality

NeoPoiesis Press
reflecting the creative drive and spirit
of the new electronic media environment

Lightning Source UK Ltd.
Milton Keynes UK
29 March 2010

152021UK00002B/2/P